What's the Issue?

WHAT ARE TRADE WARS?

By Sophie Washburne

KidHaven PUBLISHING

Published in 2020 by
KidHaven Publishing, an Imprint of Greenhaven Publishing, LLC
353 3rd Avenue
Suite 255
New York, NY 10010

Designer: Deanna Paternostro
Editor: Jennifer Lombardo

Photo credits: Cover (top) Studio concept/Shutterstock.com; cover (bottom) VP Photo Studio/Shutterstock.com; p. 5 (main) STR/AFP/Getty Images; p. 5 (inset) Goran Bogicevic/Shutterstock.com; p. 7 Everett Historical/Shutterstock.com; p. 9 (main) Tupungato/Shutterstock.com; p. 9 (inset) Robert Voight/Shutterstock.com; p. 11 DeAgostini/Getty Images; p. 13 Dorothea Lange/Keystone/Getty Images; p. 15 Artyom Ivanov/TASS via Getty Images; p. 17 (main) Sean Pavone/Shutterstock.com; p. 17 (inset) Brent Hofacker/Shutterstock.com; p. 19 (main) Viktorija Reuta/Shutterstock.com; p. 19 (inset) Kazuhiro NOGI—Pool/Getty Images; p. 21 -strizh-/Shutterstock.com.

Library of Congress Cataloging-in-Publication Data

Names: Washburne, Sophie, author.
Title: What are trade wars? / Sophie Washburne.
Description: New York : KidHaven Publishing, [2020] | Series: What's the issue? | Includes bibliographical references and index. | Audience: Ages 8. | Audience: Grades 2-3.
Identifiers: LCCN 2019035054 (print) | LCCN 2019035055 (ebook) | ISBN 9781534532229 (library binding) | ISBN 9781534532311 (paperback) | ISBN 9781534532427 (set) | ISBN 9781534532250 (ebook)
Subjects: LCSH: Protectionism–Juvenile literature. | Tariff–Juvenile literature. | International trade–Juvenile literature. | Commercial policy–Juvenile literature.
Classification: LCC HF1713 .L636 2020 (print) | LCC HF1713 (ebook) | DDC 382/.73–dc23
LC record available at https://lccn.loc.gov/2019035054
LC ebook record available at https://lccn.loc.gov/2019035055

Printed in the United States of America

Some of the images in this book illustrate individuals who are models. The depictions do not imply actual situations or events.

CPSIA compliance information: Batch #BW20KL: For further information contact Greenhaven Publishing LLC, New York, New York at 1-844-317-7404.

Please visit our website, www.greenhavenpublishing.com. For a free color catalog of all our high-quality books, call toll free 1-844-317-7404 or fax 1-844-317-7405.

CONTENTS

What's Trade?

Before you can understand what a trade war is, you need to understand trade. You might trade an apple for your friend's carrots at lunch. This is also sometimes called a swap, and it doesn't cost any money. However, when countries talk about trading with each other, they mean buying and selling things.

When one country sells something to another country, that product is called an export. When it buys something, that's an import. Exports and imports can be goods, such as food. They can also be services. For example, if someone from the United States travels to another country, they're spending money in that country on things such as hotels. This is a service called tourism.

Facing the Facts

Soybeans are one of the main exports of the United States, and machines—including computers—are one of its main imports.

China exports goods, including guitars and clothing, to many countries, including the United States. During a trade war, exporting becomes harder to do. What are trade wars, and why do we need to learn about them? Keep reading to find out!

A Different Kind of War

When you think of war, you probably think of guns and bombs. However, trade wars are fought with money, and there isn't really a winner or loser.

A trade war starts when one country makes it harder for other countries to sell their goods and services to the people who live there. This is done with tariffs and quotas. A tariff is a tax the government puts on certain imported goods, making it more expensive for people to buy those goods. A quota is a limit on the goods a country can import or export during a certain period of time.

Facing the Facts

Some people think a tariff is a tax on other countries, but it's actually a tax the government puts on its own people. For example, if the United States puts a tariff on avocados from Mexico, Americans will have to pay the tax, not Mexicans.

Unlike other wars, such as the American Civil War (shown here), trade wars don't have battles that are easily seen. You can only see their effects.

Why Do Trade Wars Happen?

Trade wars often start because of protectionism, which is the idea that a country needs to keep its own goods and services safe from **competition** with another country. The idea is that if an import gets too expensive, people will start getting the same good or service from someone in their own country.

Other countries sometimes get mad about this because it means they make less money on their exports, and the people who made those goods might lose their jobs. To **retaliate**, they might put tariffs or quotas on imports from the country that did it first. Then, the first country might get mad and retaliate again! It can keep going this way for a long time.

8

Facing the Facts

Sometimes a trade war involves more than two countries. In the early 1960s, both France and Germany put high tariffs on imported American chickens. The United States retaliated by putting tariffs on French and German goods.

When the United States puts tariffs and quotas on imports, it's because the government wants people to buy more things that are made in America.

Getting Worse

If countries keep retaliating against each other, a trade war can get very bad. Imagine you're in a fight with someone and your best friend stops talking to <u>that</u> person too. That's what it's like when other countries join a trade war to support their allies, or friends.

Another way a trade war can go from bad to worse is if two countries keep putting more and more tariffs on each other's goods. This can affect the **economies** of those countries and cause many businesses to lose money and many workers to lose their jobs. In the worst cases, a trade war can lead to a real war.

Facing the Facts

The American Revolution—the war Americans fought to win their independence from Great Britain—was partially caused by a trade war.

The Boston Tea Party is the name for an event that took place in 1773 in which American colonists threw British tea into Boston Harbor to protest the tariffs Great Britain put on imported tea. This was a step on the road to the American Revolution.

Not New

There have been trade wars throughout history. One of the most well-known trade wars in U.S. history was started by a law called the Smoot-Hawley Tariff Act of 1930. President Herbert Hoover, along with lawmakers Reed Smoot and Willis Hawley, put tariffs on **agricultural** and other imports. Other countries retaliated with their own tariffs.

This act was supposed to help American farmers and other people who were having trouble making enough money during the Great Depression. Instead, it started a trade war that made it even harder for Americans to make ends meet. The tariffs were lowered in 1934 after a different law was passed.

Facing the Facts

The Great Depression was a period of economic problems in the United States and much of the world that began in 1929 and left millions without work in the 1930s.

Along with economic problems, many Americans faced **environmental** problems during the Great Depression. Shown here is a family leaving their home because of a long **drought**.

At War with China

In 2018, President Donald Trump announced a tariff on many imports from China. In response, China placed its own tariffs on American imports. The United States retaliated by making the tariffs higher. China did the same, and the **cycle** of retaliation continued into 2019.

Trump once said that trade wars could be good. However, according to the *Washington Post* newspaper, this trade war has created some jobs for Americans but has also cost American **consumers** a lot of money. Economists, or people who study the economy, have said it could be bad for the whole world if it keeps going.

Facing the Facts

Some American businesses own factories in China. Because of the trade war, many have moved their factories to other countries—but not back to the United States.

President Donald Trump and Xi Jinping, the president of China, have tried to talk about ways to end their trade war, but as of 2019, they haven't been able to reach an agreement.

Fighting with Our Neighbors

In 2018, President Trump put tariffs on two metals—steel and aluminum—imported from Mexico and Canada. Both countries retaliated with tariffs on American goods. For example, Canada put a tariff on American maple syrup. In 2019, Trump said he would put a tariff on all Mexican imports—not just metals.

Arizona, Michigan, and Texas get a lot of their imports from Mexico. High tariffs mean people who live in these states might not be able to afford some things anymore. This is an example of the way trade wars can cause problems for everyday people.

Facing the Facts 🔍

Most people know a lot of America's avocados come from Mexico, but not many know that the top Mexican exports to the United States as of 2019 are cars and car parts.

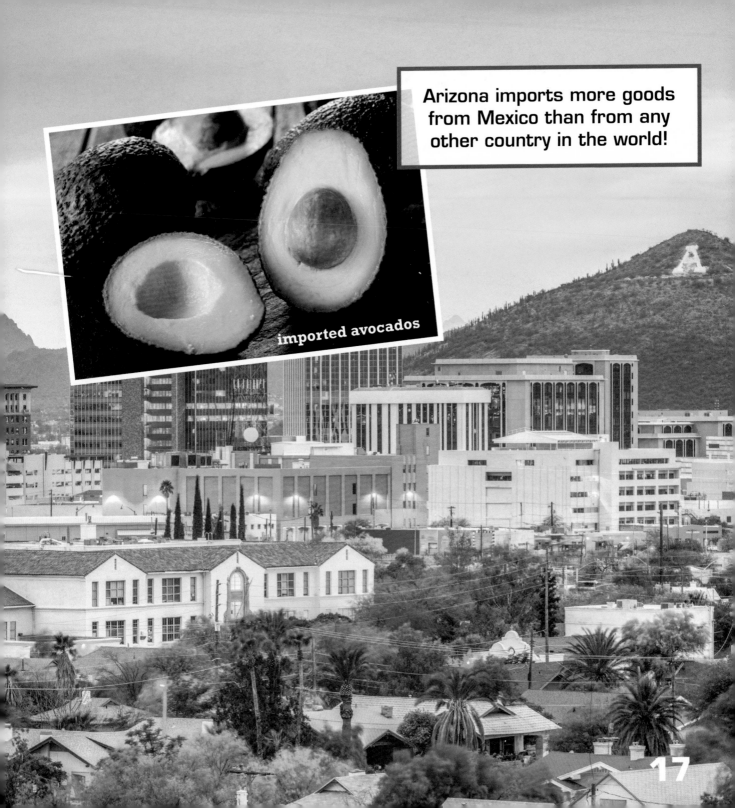

Arizona imports more goods from Mexico than from any other country in the world!

imported avocados

Ending Trade Wars

Stopping a trade war takes a lot of time and work. All of the countries involved need to be willing to talk about their problems so they can make a deal that's good for everyone.

One way countries work with each other is by going to the Group of 20 (G20) meeting each year. This is where world leaders can talk about economics and try to fix problems. This can be really hard, though! Think about a time when you had to do a group project in school. Did everyone have a different opinion about the best way to do things? That's what it's like when a lot of countries try to work together.

Facing the Facts

At the G20 meeting, countries also talk about things such as **climate** change and women's rights.

Members of G20

 Australia

 Argentina

 Turkey

 Japan

 Canada

 Germany

 Brazil

 UK

 South Africa

 France

 Italy

 Saudi Arabia

 India

 Indonesia

 China

 Mexico

 Russia

 EU

 South Korea

 USA

The G20 meeting has that name because it involves 19 countries (shown here) as well as the European Union, which represents many countries in Europe.

Taking Action

Understanding trade wars is the first step toward taking action. Decide how you feel about them. Do you think they're good or bad for the economy? Why do you feel this way? Make sure you have good reasons for your opinion; don't just repeat what you hear people on the news say.

Sometimes people talk about "voting with their dollars." This means buying things from businesses you want to support. If there's something you want to buy, look at the stores that are selling it and think about how they do business. If you don't like what one store is doing, you can **boycott** it and spend your money somewhere else.

Facing the Facts

Chick-fil-A, Amazon, FedEx, and the National Football League (NFL) are just a few of the companies and **organizations** that have been boycotted at one point or another.

WHAT CAN YOU DO?

Buy American-made goods if you want to support American workers.

Think about where your money goes when you buy something.

Write to government leaders if you feel strongly about continuing or ending a trade war.

Boycott companies if you don't like how they do business.

Ask a well-informed adult about their opinions on this topic.

Learn more about trade and the economy.

Learning more about trade wars and economics is an important part of becoming an informed, or educated, consumer and citizen. However, there are also other ways you can get involved with this issue.

GLOSSARY

agricultural: Having to do with farming.

boycott: To stop buying or using the goods and services of a business as a way to protest or to force the business to make certain changes.

climate: The weather over a long period of time.

competition: The act of trying to get or win something that someone else is also trying to get or win.

consumers: People who purchase goods or services.

cycle: A set of events or actions that happen over and over in the same order.

drought: A long period of time with little or no rain.

economy: The way in which goods and services are made, sold, and used in a country or area.

environmental: Having to do with the natural world.

organization: A group that is formed for a particular purpose.

retaliate: To do something bad to someone who has hurt you or treated you badly.

FOR MORE INFORMATION

WEBSITES

Ducksters: Economics

www.ducksters.com/money/economics.php

This website teaches the basics of economics, which is an important part of understanding trade wars.

IMF: Trading Around the World

www.imf.org/external/np/exr/center/students/trade

In this game on the International Monetary Fund (IMF) website, players represent a country and try to work around trade barriers to make deals with other countries.

BOOKS

Carr, Aaron. *World Trade.* New York, NY: AV2 by Weigl, 2015.

Kenney, Karen Latchana, and Steve Stankiewicz. *Economics Through Infographics.* Minneapolis, MN: Lerner Publications, 2015.

Mikic, Mia. *International Trade.* London, UK: Macmillan Education, Ltd., 2016.

INDEX